道

The WAY

道德經

老子

The Eternal Way of Profound Virtue

A new translation of the

Tao Te Ching — Lao tzu

by

Roger Charles Warren

R&B Enterprises
PO Box 1040
Westcliffe CO 81252
rnbwarren777@gmail.com

copyright © 1993 - 2021
Roger Charles Warren
ISBN 978-1-304-61679-1
The Eternal Way of Profound Virtue
1. Taoism; Tao Te Ching 2. Lao Tzu 3. The Way

If you use it, give proper credit.
If you prosper from it, share with others.

woodcut and calligraphy by
R.C. Warren

To Mark Wilson,
who found the way through not looking for it.

Foreword

In creating this translation, my initial goal was to create what I had been looking for as I continued along my Path. As I studied the Tao, it became clear to me that most translations of the Tao Teh Ching are the products of self serving scholars who seem more interested in attempting to prove their intelligence through the use of obscure words and endless bibliographies, than in communicating the truth to common people.

Lao Tzu said "My words are very easy to understand," but if you have to wade through extensive notes and commentary, how successful is the translation?

Important to me in this translation was that it be readable, understandable, and accurate. Only you can say if I was successful.

With this edition, I have also attempted to produce a work of asthetic pleasure. It is my heartfelt hope that people will genuinely enjoy reading and rereading this translation, and turn to it as I do for wisdom and faith.

May your path be smooth and direct.

道經

Book One

Upper Part

Tao Ching

一章

道可道，非常道。名可名，非常名。無名天地之始。有名萬物之母。故常無，欲以觀其妙。常有，欲以觀其徼。此兩者，同出而異名。同謂之玄。玄之又玄。衆妙之門。

ONE

The Way that can be called the Way
     is not the Eternal Way.
A name which can be named
     is not the Eternal Name.

That which is nameless is the beginning of all things.
Names came from the mother of all things.

Ever desireless, one can see the deepest mysteries.
Filled with desire, one sees only the outer manifestations.
The two spring from the same source,
     but have different names;
This unity is the mystery.

From mysterious darkness into mysterious darkness
Is the gateway to the essence of spirituality.

二章

天下皆知美之爲美，斯惡已。皆知善之爲善，斯不善已。

故有無相生，難易相成，長短相較，高下相傾，音聲相和，

前後相隨。是以聖人處無爲之事，行不言之教，萬物作

焉而不辭，生而不有，爲而不恃，功成而弗居。夫唯弗居，

是以不去。

Two

The world under heaven sees beauty as beauty,
  only because there is ugliness.
We recognize that which is good as good,
  only because there is evil.

Life and death are cycles of one another.
Difficulty and ease compliment each other.
Long and short contrast each other.
High and low are relative of each other.
Music and noise harmonize with each other.
Past and future follow one another.

Therefore, the wisest one achieves without doing,
Teaches without speaking.
And the many things continue to exist, regardless.
Creating without possessing;
Accomplishing without taking credit;
Succeeding without prideful acknowledgement;
In that way, the accomplishment lasts forever.

三章

不尚賢使民不爭。不貴難得之貨使民不爲盜。不見可欲使民心不亂。是以聖人之治虛其心實其腹弱其志強其骨。常使民無知無欲。使夫知者不敢爲也。爲無爲則無不治。

THREE

Absence of rewards prevents conflicts.
By not collecting riches, we prevent robbery.
By ignoring useless desires, we prevent
   misdirection of the heart.

Therefore, the most prudent rulers
      will still beating hearts,
      while filling stomachs;
Calm ambitions, while strengthening bones.

People with clear minds but no desires
   Cannot be distracted by clever interference.

By not governing the people,
They will govern themselves.

四章

道冲而用之或不盈淵兮似萬物之宗挫其銳解其紛
和其光同其塵湛兮似或存吾不知誰之子象帝之先

FOUR

The Eternal Way is a vessel which can
  never be emptied nor filled.

Oh! So deep! It must be the parent of all things!

Blunting the sharpness,
Untangling the knot,
Softening the glare,
Becoming one with the earth;

Through the depths, it becomes visible.
How could it have been born?
For it has no parents.

五章

天地不仁，以萬物為芻狗。聖人不仁，以百姓為芻狗。天地之間，其猶橐籥乎。虛而不屈，動而愈出。多言數窮，不如守中。

FIVE

Heaven and earth are without favor;
They treat the many things like scare-crows.
The wisest ones are also without favor;
They treat the people like scarecrows.

The universe between heaven and earth
   is like a bellows;
Empty, yet never exausted.
The more it is used, the more it yields.

Say more by speaking less.
Hold fast to the center.

六章

谷神不死，是謂玄牝。玄牝之門，是謂天地根。緜緜若存。用之不勤。

SIX

The spirit of the valley will live forever.
She is the woman; the mystery of motherhood.
Her doorway is the origin of both heaven
    and earth.

A wisp barely seen,
The more she gives, the more she offers.

七章

天長地久。天地所以能長且久者。以其不自生。故能長生。是以聖人後其身而身先。外其身而身存。非以其無私邪。故能成其私。

SEVEN

Heaven and earth shall last forever.
How can they last forever?
Because they were not born,
And therefore cannot die.

The wisest ones stay behind,
And are thus ahead;
They surrender themselves,
And therefore the self is preserved.

Is it not through selfless action
That we attain self-fulfillment?

八章

上善若水。水善利萬物而不爭。處眾人之所惡。故幾於道。居善地。心善淵。與善仁。言善信。正善治。事善能。動善時。夫唯不爭、故無尤。

EIGHT

The highest good is like water.
It gives life to the many things without trying.
It runs to where we would not walk,
And therefore approaches the Eternal Way.

For your home, choose the earth well.
When delving into the mind, go deep into the heart.
With others, treat them well and kind.
In speaking, use the truth.
If ruling, be just.
While serving, be competent.
In action, be aware of the timing.

Without conflict, there is no blame.

九章

持而盈之不如其已揣而梲之不可長保金玉滿堂莫之能守富貴而驕自遺其咎功遂身退天之道。

28

NINE

Better to have a full cup
    than a cup runneth over.
A blade can be honed to only so sharp
    before it becomes useless.

Fill your halls with gold and jade,
    and soon, no one can protect them.
With wealth and pride, disaster follows.

When the job is done — stop working.
This is the Eternal Way.

十章

載營魄，抱一能無離乎。專氣致柔，能嬰兒乎。滌除玄覽，能無疵乎。愛民治國，能無知乎。天門開闔，能無雌乎。明白四達，能無為乎。生之畜之。生而不有。為而不恃，長而不宰。是謂玄德。

TEN

While you bring the body and the living soul
    together as one,
By vitalizing your soul, can you become
    as supple as a newborn babe?
While cleaning the mirror of mystery
    will you leave no blemish?
Can you love the people while governing
    without deceptive cleverness?

As the gates of heaven open and close,
Can you stay to the side of a woman?
When your understanding goes in all four directions,
Can you remain still?

Giving birth and then nourishing;
Creating, yet not possessing;
Guiding without taking credit;
Leading without dominating;

This is the Profound Virtue.

十一章

三十輻共一轂。當其無、有車之用。埏埴以爲器當其無、有器之用。鑿戶牖以爲室當其無、有室之用故有之以爲利無之以爲用。

ELEVEN

Thirty spokes form one hole at the hub.
It is this empty space which makes the wheel useful.
Shape clay into a bowl.
Its empty space is what makes it useful.
Cut out doors and windows in a room.
The usefulness is from the empty space.

Thus, what exists becomes useful
By what does not.

十二章

五色令人目盲。五音令人耳聾。五味令人口爽。馳騁畋獵令人心發狂難得之貨令人行妨。是以聖人爲腹不爲目。故去彼取此

TWELVE

Five colors blind the eye.
Five tones deafen the ear.
Five tastes dull the tongue.
Racing and hunting madden the mind.
Treasures will lead one astray.

And so, the wisest ones are guided
   by what they feel, not what they see.

To let go of one, in favor of the other.

十三章

寵辱若驚貴大患若身。何謂寵辱若驚寵為下得之若驚失之若驚是謂寵辱若驚。何謂貴大患若身吾所以有大患者為吾有身及吾無身吾有何患故貴以身為天下若可寄天下愛以身為天下若可託天下。

THIRTEEN

Fortune and misfortune are of equal concern.
Accept tragedy as your own.

What is meant by "Fortune and misfortune are
    of equal concern?"
Fortune creates the concern of losing it.
This is why "Fortune and misfortune are
    of equal concern."

How can you "Accept tragedy as your own?"
We think of ourselves as only our bodies,
But, without our bodies, how can we have pain?
Thus, one who loves all things as the self
    Can be trusted with all things.
One who loves the world as the self
    Can be trusted to take care of the world.

十四章

視之不見名曰夷。聽之不聞名曰希。搏之不得名曰微。此三者不可致詰故混而爲一其上不皦其下不昧。繩繩不可名復歸於無物是謂無狀之狀無物之象是謂惚恍。迎之不見其首隨之不見其後。執古之道以御今之有能知古始是謂道紀。

FOURTEEN

Look to see what cannot be seen.
It is invisible.
Listen to hear what cannot be heard.
It is subtle.
Grasp to hold what is beyond reach.
It is intangible.
These three concepts are beyond words,
Yet they come together as one.

The top is not bright.
The bottom is not dark.
Unbroken yet indescribable, it moves on,
Returning into nothingness.
It is the form of the formless —
The image of the imageless.
It is called "beyond comprehension."

It comes, you see not its face.
It goes, you see not its back.
Seek the ancient Way to take care of the present.

One who can see the origin of time
Is connected with the Eternal Way.

十五章

古之善爲士者微妙玄通深不可識夫唯不可識故強
爲之容豫焉若冬涉川猶兮若畏四鄰儼兮其若容渙
兮若冰之將釋敦兮其若樸曠兮其若谷混兮其若濁
孰能濁以靜之徐清孰能安以久動之徐生保此道者
不欲盈夫唯不盈故能蔽不新成。

40

FIFTEEN

The ancient wise ones were subtle and spiritual,
Profound and penetrating.
Their wisdom was far from comprehension.
Because it was far from comprehension,
    we have only a vague picture.
Careful, as one crossing a winter stream;
Alert, and aware of danger;
Courteous, like a visitor;
Yielding, like melting ice;
Simple and pure, like uncut wood;
Open, like a gorge;
Murky, as muddy water.
Who can be patient while the water clears?
Who can relax until the moment to spring alive?

Those who follow the Eternal Way
    do not seek fulfillment.
Without need of new things,
They are complete.

十六章

致虛極守靜篤萬物並作吾以觀復夫物芸芸各復歸其根。歸根曰靜。是謂復命復命曰常。知常曰明不知常妄作凶。知常容。容乃公。公乃王王乃天。天乃道。道乃久。沒身不殆。

SIXTEEN

By continually emptying yourself of everything,
You can acheive absolute peace and tranquility.
The many things of life rise and fall,
While we watch them return once again;
They grow and flourish,
And then lay stalk and seed to the roots.
Returning to the roots is tranquility,
Which is the way of everything,
And this never changes.
Insight of this constancy is enlightenment.
To ignore it is to invite disaster.
Seeing this constancy, the mind is opened;
An opened mind opens the heart;
An opened heart provides exemplary leadership;
Leading others toward heaven,
And toward the Infinite Way,
Which is to become infinite.
As the physical body passes on,
The Infinite Way carries on.

十七章

太上下知有之。其次親而譽之。其次畏之。其次侮之。信不足焉有不信焉悠兮其貴言功成事遂百姓皆謂我自然。

SEVENTEEN

The best leaders are known the least.
There are those who are known and loved,
And come the ones who are feared,
And the ones who are put to shame,

But those who cannot trust are not trusted.

Then, when a good leader, with little talk,
Accomplishes the goal.
The people say "<u>we</u> did it!"

十八章

大道廢有仁義慧智出有大僞六親不和有孝慈國家昏亂有忠臣

EIGHTEEN

And so, when sight is lost of the Eternal Way,
First rise kindness and justice, and
Then, knowledge and cleverness.
This is the birth of hypocrisy.

When the family is not in peace
Comes the honor of the parents.
When the country is in chaos,
Come the ministers.

十九章

絕聖棄智，民利百倍。絕仁棄義，民復孝慈。絕巧棄利，盜賊無有。此三者以爲文不足，故令有所屬。見素抱樸，少私寡欲。

NINETEEN

To give up on saints and abandon scholars
Would be a hundred times better for everyone.

Give up tolerance and abandon righteousness,
And people will rediscover kindness and love.

Give up cleverness and abandon greed,
And thieves and bandits will also disappear.

These three statements show that words alone
   are not enough.
People should embrace something more lasting:
Seek the plain and grasp the uncut wood.
Think not of yourself, and diminish desires.

Give up learnedness and you abandon worry.

二十章

絕學無憂唯之與阿、相去幾何。善之與惡、相去若何。人之所畏不可不畏、荒兮其未央哉、眾人熙熙如享太牢。如登春臺、我獨泊兮其未兆、如嬰兒之未孩、儽儽兮若無所歸。眾人皆有餘、而我獨若遺、我愚人之心也哉、沌沌兮、俗人昭昭、我獨昏昏、俗人察察、我獨悶悶、澹兮其若海、飂兮若無止、眾人皆有以、而我獨頑似鄙、我獨異於人、而貴食母。

50

TWENTY

How much difference is there between yes and no?
How much distance is between good and evil?
Must I fear what others fear? Nonsense!
While other people are happy, as if enjoying
    a great feast,
Or stepping onto a spring terrace,
I am adrift and without a clue.
Like a baby who has not yet learned to smile,
I am alone without a home to return to.

Others have more than they need,
While I am left alone with nothing.
I have the mind of a fool, filled with confusion.
While others are bright and clear,
I alone am dim and dull.
While others are clever and aware,
I alone am vague and dumb,
    Drifting like the sea, and restless like the wind.

While others are busy with purpose,
I alone am stubborn without reason.
I am different from them.
I prefer to be fed by the eternal mother.

二十一章

孔德之容惟道是從。道之爲物惟恍惟惚。惚兮恍兮其中有象。恍兮惚兮其中有物。窈兮冥兮其中有精。其精甚真。其中有信。自古及今其名不去以閱衆甫吾何以知衆甫之狀哉以此。

52

TWENTY ONE

Profound Virtue is found in the Eternal Way
And the Way alone.
The Eternal Way is elusive and intangible.
Oh, how intangible and elusive,
Yet within it is image.
Oh, how elusive and intangible,
Yet within it is form.
How empty and dark!
Yet within it is essence.
This essence is very real,
And withstands the test of faith.
From the beginning of time until now,
Its name has persisted.
Through this is brought forth the foremost of all things.
How can we know the foremost of all things?
Through This.

二十二章

曲則全枉則直窪則盈敝則新少則得多則惑是以聖人抱一爲天下式不自見故明不自是故彰不自伐故有功不自矜故長夫唯不爭故天下莫能與之爭古之所謂曲則全者豈虛言哉誠全而歸之。

TWENTY TWO

To bend is not to break.

To be crooked is to be straightened.
To be empty is to be filled.
To wear out is to become new.
Having little is to gain.
Having much is to be confused.

Therefore, the wisest ones embrace the One.
And are thus an example to the world.
By not calling attention, one shines brilliantly.
By not seeking justification, one is justified.
By not bragging, one is recognized.
By not boasting, one can endure.
By not competing, one is without competition.

Therefore, the ancient saying,
"To bend is not to break" is not meaningless.
Be sincerely whole,
And all shall return intact.

二十三章

希言自然故飄風不終朝。驟雨不終日。孰爲此者天地。天地尚不能久而況於人乎故從事於道者道者同於道德者同於德失者同於失同於道者道亦樂得之。同於德者德亦樂得之。同於失者失亦樂得之。信不足焉，有不信焉。

TWENTY THREE

To talk little is natural.

Strong winds do not last all morning.
A cloudburst does not last all day.
Where do they come from? Heaven and earth!
If heaven and earth cannot bring about endurance,
    then how can mankind?

Therefore, one who follows the Eternal Way
Is at One with the Way.
One who is of Virtue is at one with Profound Virtue.
One who loses the Way of Virtue is lost.
One who is of the Way is happily greeted by the Way.
One who is of Virtue is happily greeted by Virtue.
One who loses is happily greeted by loss.

Those who do not trust enough
Cannot be trusted.

二十四章

企者不立跨者不行自見者不明自是者不彰自伐者
無功自矜者不長其在道也曰餘食贅行物或惡之故
有道者不處。

TWENTY FOUR

One who tiptoes is unsteady.
One who strides cannot keep the pace.
One who shows off is not brilliant.
One who is self justified loses respect.
One who brags will not endure long.
Along the Way,
This is spoiled food and excess baggage,
And not in our nature of happiness,
And thus should be avoided
By those who follow the Eternal Way.

二十五章

有物混成先天地生寂兮寥兮獨立不改周行而不殆。可以為天下母吾不知其名。字之曰道强為之名曰大。大曰逝逝曰遠遠曰反故道大天大地大王亦大。域中有四大而王居其一焉人法地地法天天法道道法自然。

TWENTY FIVE

There is something mysteriously completed,
Born before heaven and earth.
In silence and in emptiness,
It stands alone and unchanging,
Forever turning.
It could be the mother of all things.
Knowing not its name, call it "the Way."
If made to describe it, call it great.
Being great, it flows onward.
Flowing onward, it is far reaching.
Being far reaching, it thus returns.
Therefore, the Way is great.
Heaven is great.
Earth is great.
And the true leaders are also great.
There are four great things in the universe,
And true leaders are one of them.
People follow the earth.
The earth follows heaven.
Heaven follows the Way.
The Way follows what is natural.

二十六章

重爲輕根。靜爲躁君。是以聖人終日行不離輜重。雖有榮觀、燕處超然。奈何萬乘之主而以身輕天下。輕則失本。躁則失君。

TWENTY SIX

Heavy is the root of the light.
Stillness rules over unrest.

Therefore, the wisest one, while traveling all day,
Does not lose sight of necessities,
And although in the midst of a teaming estate,
Remains calmly above it.

Should the ruler of ten thousand chariots
Behave lightly before the public?

When light, the root is lost.
When restless, the rule is lost.

二十七章

善行無轍迹。善言無瑕讁。善數不用籌策。善閉無關楗而不可開。善結無繩約而不可解。是以聖人常善救人，故無棄人。常善救物，故無棄物。是謂襲明。故善人者不善人之師。不善人者善人之資。不貴其師不愛其資雖智大迷。是謂要妙。

TWENTY SEVEN

A good traveler leaves no tracks.
A good speaker makes no slips.
A good memory requires no tally.
A good seal requires no lock,
Yet once closed, cannot be opened.
Good binding requires no cord,
Yet cannot be undone.

Therefore, the wisest one is good at saving all,
And abandons none;
Is good at saving all things,
And abandons nothing.

This is called "harmonizing with all things."

Therefore, who is good?
The teacher of the bad.
Who is bad?
One deserving attention from the good.
If the teacher is not valued,
And the student not loved,
Confusion results, regardless of knowledge.
This is the essence of the mystery.

二十八章

知其雄，守其雌，爲天下谿。爲天下谿，常德不離，復歸於嬰兒。知其白，守其黑，爲天下式。爲天下式，常德不忒，復歸於無極。知其榮，守其辱，爲天下谷。爲天下谷，常德乃足，復歸於樸。樸散則爲器。聖人用之，則爲官長。故大制不割。

66

TWENTY EIGHT

Know the masculine, but keep to the feminine.
Be the valley of the universe.
As the valley of the universe,
Ever unswerving from virtue,
Return to childhood.

Know the brilliant,
But keep to the tarnished.
Be an example to the whole world!
As an example to the whole world,
Ever true to your virtue,
Return to the infinite.

Know honor, but keep humble.
Be the valley for the whole world.
As the valley of the whole world,
Being ever true to integrity is enough
To return to the simplicity of uncut wood.

When wood is cut, it becomes useful.
The wise one makes use of it, and becomes ruler.
In so doing, the greatest carver cuts little.

二十九章

將欲取天下而爲之。吾見其不得已。天下神器不可爲也。爲者敗之。執者失之。故物或行或隨或歔或吹或強或羸或挫或隳。是以聖人去甚去奢去泰。

TWENTY NINE

There are those who wish to take the universe
To improve upon it,
But this cannot be done.

The whole universe is sacred.
It cannot be improved upon.
One who tries to improve it shall ruin it.
One who wishes to possess it shall lose it.

At times, some are ahead and some are behind;
Some breathe gently and some are out of breath;
Some are strong and some are weak;
Some get up and some fall down.

Therefore, the wisest one
Avoids extremes, excesses and arrogance.

三十章

以道佐人主者，不以兵強天下。其事好還。師之所處，荊棘生焉。大軍之後，必有凶年。善者果而已。不敢以取強。果而勿矜。果而勿伐。果而勿驕。果而不得已。果而勿強。物壯則老。是謂不道。不道早已。

THIRTY

Those who show the Way to a leader
Do not use force.
Force only causes resistance.
Where an army has been only thorns grow.
Famine follows the war.
Do what should be done without force.

Get it done without fanfare.
Get it done without boasting.
Get it done without pride.
Overcome obstacles when neccesary,
But not through force.

One cannot force maturity.
This is not the Way.
By going the wrongway,
One meets an early end.

三十一章

夫佳兵者不祥之器物或惡之故有道者不處君子居則貴左·用兵則貴右兵者不祥之器非君子之器不得已而用之恬淡爲上勝而不美而美之者是樂殺人夫樂殺人者則不可以得志於天下矣·吉事尚左凶事尚右偏將軍居左上將軍居右言以喪禮處之殺人之眾以哀悲泣之戰勝·以喪禮處之

THIRTY ONE

Fine weapons invoke fear,
And are thus hated.
Therefore, those who know the way
Do not use them.
The wise one goes one way,
while the soldier goes another.

As instruments of fear, the wise one
Will use weapons only when given no choice,
    and with distain,
Preffering peace and quiet.
Victory is no celebration.
One who celebrates victory, celebrates killing.
One who celebrates killing will never be fulfilled.

Celebrations are conducted to one side;
Mournful occasions are conducted to the other.
A commander moves his army from the other side;
Thus, a war is conducted like a funeral.
When many are killed,
They should be mourned with great sorrow.
And so, a victory should be regarded like a funeral.

三十二章

道常無名樸雖小天下莫能臣也。侯王若能守之，萬物將自賓。天地相合，以降甘露，民莫之令而自均。始制有名。名亦既有，夫亦將知止，知止可以不殆譬道之在天下。猶川谷之於江海。

THIRTY TWO

The Eternal Way is infinitely undefinable.
Although small, like a piece of uncut wood,
It cannot be contained.
If all the rulers could follow the Way,
The entire world would fall into order.
Heaven and earth would be united
By a sweetly falling rain.
Needing no longer to be ruled,
The entire natural order would fall into place.

In the beginning, the whole was divided;
And so the many parts needed names.
With so many names,
When is the time to stop?
By knowing when to stop,
One escapes trouble.
The world seeks the Way
Like a river flowing to the sea.

三十三章

知人者智自知者明。勝人者有力自勝者強知足者富

强行者有志不失其所者久死而不忘者壽。

THIRTY THREE

Knowing others is knowledge.
Knowing the self is true enlightenment.

Controlling others requires force.
Controlling yourself requires true power of the will.

One who is content with what is,
Is truly rich.

Perseverance shows will power.
Constancy will endure,
Even beyond death, existing forever.

三十四章

大道氾兮其可左右。萬物恃之而生而不辭。功成不名有。衣養萬物而不爲主。常無欲,可名於小,萬物歸焉而不爲主,可名爲大,以其終不自爲大。故能成其大。

THIRTY FOUR

The Great and Eternal Way is everywhere:
 On the one side, and on the other.
It gives life to all things, and then frees them.
It completes the task silently, making no claims.

It feeds and protects all things,
But is not their ruler.
Forever free of desire, it is very meek.

All things return to it,
Yet, it is not their ruler.
It is very great.

Being unaware of its greatness
Makes it truly great.

三十五章

執大象,天下往。往而不害,安平太。樂與餌,過客止。道之出口,淡乎其無味,視之不足見,聽之不足聞,用之不足既。

THIRTY FIVE

The world soon gathers around one
Who has a great image.
There, they escape harm,
And find peace and harmony.

One passing by may be attracted
By music and good food.
The Way, by comparison,
When passing through the mouth
Is bland and without savor.

Although it cannot be seen or heard,
Its uses are limitless.

三十六章

將欲歙之,必固張之。將欲弱之,必固強之。將欲廢之,必固興之。將欲奪之,必固與之。是謂微明。柔弱勝剛強。魚不可脫於淵,國之利器,不可以示人。

THIRTY SIX

In order to shrink,
One must first expand.
To be weakened,
One must first be strong.
For something to be thrown down,
It must first be raised up.
In order to receive,
One must first give.

This is called the subtle nature of the Way of life.
The soft and meek shall overcome the hard and strong.

Just as a fish cannot long endure outside the depths,
A nation cannot long endure with weapons on display.

三十七章

道常無爲而無不爲。侯王若能守之，萬物將自化。化而

欲作，吾將鎮之以無名之樸。無名之樸，夫亦將無欲。不

欲以靜，天下將自定。

THIRTY SEVEN

The Eternal Way does nothing,
Yet leaves nothing undone.

If leaders follow the Way,
Soon all things will naturally come into harmony
   of themselves.

Having done this, they will be freed from desires
By the unnamed simplicity of uncut wood.

Freedom from desire is tranquility.
This is the way the whole world will be at peace.

德
經

Book Two

Lower Part

Te Ching

三十八章

上德不德，是以有德。下德不失德，是以無德。上德無為，而無以為。下德為之，而有以為。上仁為之，而無以為。上義為之，而有以為。上禮為之，而莫之應，則攘臂而扔之。故失道而後德。失德而後仁。失仁而後義。失義而後禮。夫禮者忠信之薄而亂之首。前識者道之華而愚之始。是以大丈夫處其厚不居其薄。處其實不居其華。故去彼取此。

THIRTY EIGHT

Those of Profound Virtue do not strive to be virtuous,
And are thus truly virtuous.
Those without virtue are forever trying to appear virtuous,
And so are truly without virtue.

Those of Profound Virtue do nothing,
Yet leave nothing undone.
Those without virtue do many things,
Leaving many things undone.

When one of virtue acts, it is without selfish motivation.
When one of justice acts, it is with selfishness.
When one of ritual acts, and gets no response,
The fists are bared to use force.

Therefore, the loss of the Way is followed by virtue.
The loss of virtue is followed by justice.
The loss of justice is followed by ritual.
Ritual is depleted of faith and honesty,
And is the beginning of disarray.
Traditional ancient knowledge is only the flower of the Way,
And is the beginning of folly.

Therefore, the enlightened ones see the whole,
Not just the superficial;
The fruit, and not just the flower;
Rejecting one, in favor of the other.

三十九章

昔之得一者。天得一以清。地得一以寧。神得一以靈。谷得一以盈。萬物得一以生。侯王得一以為天下貞。其致之。天無以清將恐裂。地無以寧將恐發。神無以靈將恐歇。谷無以盈將恐竭。萬物無以生將恐滅。侯王無以貴高將恐蹶。故貴以賤為本。高以下為基。是以侯王自謂孤寡不穀。此非以賤為本邪非乎。故致數輿無輿不欲琭琭如玉珞珞如石。

THIRTY NINE

From ancient times, many things have come together as one.
By becoming One, the sky is clear.
By becoming One, the earth is firm.
By becoming One, the spirits are strong.
By becoming One, the valley is full.
By becoming One, the many things come alive.
When rulers and leaders become as one,
All under heaven flourishes.
These things are so because they are One.

That which is not clear in the sky settles to earth.
That which is not firm with the earth blows to the spirits.
That which is not strong with the spirits sinks to the valleys.
That which does not dry up, flows from the valley
     and nourishes the many things.
Then the many things grow and support their leaders.

Therefore, the humble is the root of the noble.
The low provides foundation for the high.
Rulers and leaders see themselves
As "lonely," "abandoned," and "without center."
Humility is their baggage, is it not?

The wheel is useful because it has no center.
One should not strive to be brilliant and rare as jade,
But instead, as dull and ordinary as stone.

四十章

反者道之動。弱者道之用天下萬物生於有。有生於無。

FORTY

The Eternal Way is forever returning.
To give is the Way.
All things come from something.
Yet, indeed, something comes from nothing.

四十一章

上士聞道勤而行之。中士聞道若存若亡。下士聞道大笑之。不笑不足以爲道。故建言有之。明道若昧。進道若退。夷道若纇。上德若谷。大白若辱。廣德若不足。建德若偷。質真若渝。大方無隅。大器晚成。大音希聲。大象無形。道隱無名。夫唯道善貸且成。

FORTY ONE

The good scholar hears of the Way,
    and follows the path immediately.
The average scholar hears of the Way,
    and tries to follow, but frequently becomes distracted.
A poor scholar will hear of the Way,
    and laugh out loud.
Without the laughter, this could not be the Way.

This is why it is said:
"The Path of light seems dark."
"The Path forward, returns."
"The easiest Path seems hard."
"Profound Virtue feels empty."
"The greatest purity seems defiled."
"Overflowing Virtue seems inadequate."
"Strong Virtue appears shameless."
"The honest truth seems deceptive."
"The greatest square has no corners."
"A great instrument takes time to develop."
"Great music seems difficult to hear."
"A great image has no shape."

The Path is obscure, being nameless.
It is this path alone that nourishes
And fulfills all things.

四十二章

道生一。一生二。二生三。三生萬物。萬物負陰而抱陽冲氣以爲和。人之所惡唯孤寡不穀而王公以爲稱故物或損之而益或益之而損人之所教我亦教之。强梁者不得其死吾將以爲教父。

FORTY TWO

From the Way came the One;
From the One came Two;
From the Two came Three;
And from the Three came all things.

The many things support the shadowed side,
And embrace the sunny side,
And the soul of nature comes together in harmony.

No one wants to be "lonely," "abandoned," and
   "without center,"
Yet this is how our leaders describe themselves.

Great gains come from losing,
And losing comes from gain.

What others teach, I also teach:
"One who is violent will die violently."
I take this as the basis for my teaching.

四十三章

天下之至柔，馳騁天下之至堅。無有入無間。吾是以知無爲之有益。不言之教，無爲之益，天下希及之。

FORTY THREE

The softest thing in the universe
Shall overcome the hardest thing in the universe.

Something without substance can penetrate,
Although through no openings.
This is how I know the benefit of suspending action.

Teaching without words,
And accomplishing without action
Are understood by few under heaven.

四十四章

名與身孰親。身與貨孰多得與亡孰病。是故甚愛必大費。多藏必厚亡。知足不辱知止不殆可以長久。

FORTY FOUR

Fame or self: Which is more important?
Health or money: Which is worth more?
Success or failure: Which is more damaging?

Great attachment produces the pain of detachment.
Collecting wealth produces more to lose.
One who is content is without disappointment.
By knowing when to stop, one avoids trouble,
And in this way will endure.

四十五章

大成若缺。其用不弊。大盈若沖。其用不窮。大直若屈。大巧若拙。大辯若訥。躁勝寒。靜勝熱。清靜為天下正。

FORTY FIVE

The perfect accomplishment seems unfinished,
Yet is useful forever.
Perfectly full seems empty,
Yet can never be depleted.

Perfectly straight appears twisted.
Pefect wisdom seems foolish.
Perfect eloquence seems awkward.

Activity overcomes the cold.
Stillness overcomes the heat.

Peace and tranquility
Will put the entire universe into order.

四十六章

天下有道，郤走馬以糞。天下無道，戎馬生於郊。禍莫大於不知足。咎莫大於欲得。故知足之足常足矣。

FORTY SIX

When the world follows the Way,
Race horses are used to plow fields.
When the world ignores the Way,
War horses are bred on the borders.

The greatest sin is selfish desire.
Misfortune comes from discontentment.
Disaster comes from self gain.

Therefore, one who is content to be content
Will always be content.

四十七章

不出戶，知天下。不闚牖，見天道。其出彌遠，其知彌少。是以聖人不行而知，不見而名，不爲而成。

FORTY SEVEN

Without going outside your door,
You can know all under heaven.
Without looking outside your window,
You can know the Way of heaven.

The further you travel,
The less you understand.

And so, the wisest one understands
Without traveling;
Sees without looking;
And accomplishes without doing a thing.

四十八章

為學日益為道日損損之又損以至於無為無為而無不為取天下常以無事及其有事不足以取天下。

FORTY EIGHT

Along the road to knowledge,
Every day something is picked up.

Along the way,
Every day something is put down.

Less and less, until there is nothing.
When there is nothing to do,
Nothing is left undone.

One rules the world by leaving it alone.
By interfering, one proves that the world
Is not to be ruled.

四十九章

聖人無常心。以百姓心爲心。善者吾善之。不善者吾亦善之。德善。信者吾信之。不信者吾亦信之。德信。聖人在天下歙歙爲天下渾其心。聖人皆孩之。

110

FORTY NINE

The wisest one possesses not the common mind,
But is of the mind of all others.

Being good to those who are good,
And being good also to those who are not good,
Develops the Virtue of goodness.

Having faith in those who are faithful,
And having faith also in those who are not faithful,
Develops the Virtue of faith.

The wisest one is humble and shy,
And being of the mind of the whole world,
Appears confused.
People all look and listen.
Here is the trust of a child.

五十章

出生入死。生之徒十有三。死之徒十有三。人之生動之
死地亦十有三。夫何故。以其生生之厚。蓋聞善攝生者。
陸行不遇虎兕。入軍不被甲兵。兕無所投其角。虎無所
措其爪。兵無所容其刃。夫何故。以其無死地。

FIFTY

When traveling between life and death,
Three in ten will walk with life;
Three in ten will walk with death;
And those clinging to life, yet slipping toward death,
Are also three in ten.
Why is this?
Because they value life too much.

It is said however, that there are also those
who know to walk through life without fear
    of the wild rhinoceros or tiger,
And know to enter battle without weapons.
The horn of the rhinoceros has nothing to gore,
The claws of the tiger have nothing to shred,
And the blade of the weapon has nowhere to pierce.
Why is this?
Because death has no meaning to them.

五十一章

道生之。德畜之。物形之。勢成之。是以萬物莫不尊道而貴德。道之尊德之貴夫莫之命而常自然。故道生之。德畜之長之育之亭之毒之養之覆之。生而不有。為而不恃。長而不宰是謂玄德。

FIFTY ONE

All things come from the Eternal Way,
And are then nourished by Profound Virtue.
They are born of the pysical,
But completed by the spiritual.
And so, all things respect the Way,
And honor Virtue.
The Way is respected and Virtue honored,
Not because it is mandated,
But because this is what natvarally occurs.

Therefore, all things come from the Way,
And by Virtue they are nourished,
Nurtured, developed, sustained,
Fed, sheltered, matured and protected.
It creates without taking possession;
Accomplishes without taking credit;
Guides without taking control.
This is mysterious Virtue.

五十二章

天下有始以爲天下母。既得其母以知其子。既知其子
復守其母沒身不殆。塞其兌,閉其門,終身不勤。開其兌,
濟其事,終身不救。見小曰明,守柔曰強。用其光復歸其
明。無遺身殃。是謂習常。

FIFTY TWO

The origin of the universe can be called
The Mother of all things.
By knowing the Mother,
One can also know the children.
Knowing the children, one returns to the Mother.
And so, although the body may perish,
There is no fear of death.

Close the door of the mouth,
And the windows of the senses,
And trouble cannot enter into life.
Open the mouth. interfere,
And hopelessness enters life.

Seeing the very smallest is insight.
Giving without resistance is strength.
Use brilliance to achieve insight,
And thereby escape tragedy.
This is the eternal constancy.

五十三章

使我介然有知。行於大道。唯施是畏。大道甚夷而民好徑。朝甚除。田甚蕪倉甚虛服文綵帶利劍厭飫食財貨有餘。是謂盜夸非道也哉。

FIFTY THREE

Even if I have just the slightest bit of sense,
I will walk along the great Path,
Fearing only that I might stray from it.
The great Path is smooth and straight,
Yet people prefer the side roads.

When the rulers court is decorated in splendor,
But the fields are full of weeds,
The granaries will be empty.
They wear elegant clothes,
But keep a sharp sword by their side.
They glut themselves on food and drink,
And have more wealth than they can use.
They are ruthless robbers.
This is certainly not the Way.

五十四章

善建者不拔。善抱者不脫。子孫以祭祀不輟。修之於身。其德乃真。修之於家。其德乃餘。修之於鄉。其德乃長。修之於國。其德乃豐。修之於天下。其德乃普。故以身觀身。以家觀家。以鄉觀鄉。以國觀國。以天下觀天下。吾何以知天下然哉以此。

FIFTY FOUR

The firmly established cannot be uprooted.
What is tightly embraced will not slip away.
And so, the ancestors will be honored always,
From generation to generation.

Cultivated in oneself, Virtue becomes real.
Cultivated in the family, Virtue grows.
Cultivated in the community, Virtue becomes abundant.
Cultivated in the nation, Virtue flourishes.
Cultivated in the universe, Virtue is everywhere.

Therefore, see all people as yourself;
See all families as your own family;
See all communities as your own community;
See all nations as your own nation;
And see the universe as your own universe.

How can I see the nature of the universe?
By looking through this.

五十五章

含德之厚，比於赤子。蜂蠆虺蛇不螫，猛獸不據，攫鳥不搏。骨弱筋柔而握固。未知牝牡之合而全作，精之至也。終日號而不嗄，和之至也。知和曰常，知常曰明。益生曰祥，心使氣曰强，物壯則老，謂之不道，不道早已。

FIFTY FIVE

One who has embraced Profound Virtue
Is like a newborn baby.
Wasps and snakes do not attack.
Wild beasts do not pounce.
Birds of prey do not swoop and seize.
The bones are soft and muscles weak,
But the grip is firm.
It knows nothing of the union of male and female,
Yet its organs are vital and active
With an essense of Virtue.
It wails all day without becoming hoarse.
This is the essense of harmony.

Knowing harmony daily is constancy.
Knowing constancy daily is enlightenment.

It is not wise to rush toward maturity.
Controlling vitality requires force.
One cannot force maturity.
This is not the Way.
By going the wrong way,
One meets an early end.

五十六章

知者不言言者不知。塞其兌閉其門挫其銳解其分和其光同其塵是謂玄同。故不可得而親不可得而疏不可得而利不可得而害不可得而貴不可得而賤故為天下貴。

FIFTY SIX

Those who know much talk little.
Those who talk much know little.

Close your mouth.
Shut your doors.
Blunt your sharpness.
Untangle your knots.
Soften your brightness.
Join with the dust of the earth.
This is the mysterious unity.

Upon this, one is neither intimate nor distant;
Is neither helped nor harmed;
Is not honored or humiliated;
And so has achieved the highest state
    of the universe.

五十七章

以正治國以奇用兵以無事取天下吾何以知其然哉。

以此天下多忌諱而民彌貧民多利器國家滋昏人多伎巧奇物滋起法令滋彰盜賊多有故聖人云我無爲而民自化我好靜而民自正我無事而民自富我無欲而民自樸。

FIFTY SEVEN

A nation is ruled with justice;
A war is waged with injustice;
But the universe is won without trying.
How do I know? By this:

The more restrictions and prohibitions there are,
The poorer the people become.
The more dangerous the weapons are,
The more chaotic the nation becomes.
The more clever and ingenious the people become,
The more strange events there are.
With more laws and regulations,
There are also more thieves and outlaws.

Therefore, the wisest one says:
  While I take no action, others will become transformed.
  While I enjoy the peace, others become honest.
  While I do nothing, others will become rich.
  While I have no desires, others will live a life
  As simple as uncut trees.

五十八章

其政悶悶、其民淳淳。其政察察、其民缺缺。禍兮福之所倚。福兮禍之所伏。孰知其極。其無正。正復為奇。善復為妖。人之迷其日固久。是以聖人方而不割。廉而不劌。直而不肆。光而不燿。

FIFTY EIGHT

When government is light and tolerant,
The people are happy and prosperous.
When government is heavy and oppressive,
The people are needy and sad.

Happiness depends on hardship.
Hardship hides behind happiness.
How can we know the future?
When there is no honesty,
The honest become dishonest.
Good becomes evil.
The evil of mankind has gone on and on.

Therefore, the wisest one is sharp but not cutting;
Pointed, but not penetrating;
Straight, but not strained;
Brilliant, but not blinding.

五十九章

治人事天，莫若嗇。夫唯嗇，是謂早服。早服謂之重積德。重積德，則無不克。無不克，則莫知其極。莫知其極，可以有國。有國之母，可以長久。是謂深根固柢，長生久視之道。

FIFTY NINE

In ministering to people and serving heaven,
Nothing compares to moderation.
In moderation, one follows the path
     from the beginning.
By following the path from the beginning,
One continually builds Virtue.
By continually building Virtue,
One can overcome anything.
By overcoming anything,
One knows no limits.
One who knows no limits can rule the kingdom.
By becoming one with the mother of the kingdom,
One can long endure.
This is called having deep roots
And a strong foundation.
To longevity and eternal vision,
This is the Way.

六十章

治大國若烹小鮮。以道莅天下，其鬼不神。非其鬼不神，其神不傷人。非其神不傷人，聖人亦不傷人。夫兩不相傷，故德交歸焉。

SIXTY

One should govern a large country
As if frying a small fish.
When the world is governed by the Way,
Evil spirits have no power.
Not that there is no evil power,
But this power cannot bring harm to people.
Not only does it not bring harm to people,
But the rulers also bring no harm.
Neither brings harm,
And Virtue comes to both.

六十一章

大國者下流天下之交天下之牝牝常以靜勝牡以靜為下故大國以下小國則取小國小國以下大國則取大國故或下以取或下而取大國不過欲兼畜人小國不過欲入事人夫兩者各得其所欲大者宜為下

SIXTY ONE

A great country is like a valley,
With all streams flowing into it.
This is the Eternal Female,
Where the universe comes together.

The female can overcome the male with stillness.
Being still is taking the lower position.

By taking the lower position,
The great country can occupy the small country.
Being in the lower position,
The small country receives the great country.
The great country unites by taking the lower position,
And the small country unites by remaining
    in the lower position.

The great country wants simply to grow.
The small country wants simply to serve its guests.
As they both get what they want,
It is fitting that the greater
Take the lower position

六十二章

道者萬物之奧善人之寶不善人之所保美言可以市。
尊行可以加人人之不善何棄之有故立天子置三公
雖有拱璧以先駟馬不如坐進此道古之所以貴此道
者何不曰以求得有罪以免邪故爲天下貴。

SIXTY TWO

The Way is the well from which all things spring.
It is a treasure for the good,
And a shelter for the bad.

A good word can buy honor;
Making a gift of a good deed gains respect;
Yet even one who is bad should not be abandoned.

And so, when the sovereign is crowned,
And the three high ministers installed,
A gift of jade pulled by four fine horses
Does not compare to showing them the Way
   without the effort.

Why has the Way been so valued for so long?
Is it not because those who seek, find,
And those who are guilty are forgiven?
This is why it is so treasured by all under heaven.

六十三章

為無為。事無事。味無味。大小多少。報怨以德。圖難於其易。為大於其細。天下難事必作於易。天下大事必作於細。是以聖人終不為大。故能成其大。夫輕諾必寡信。多易必多難。是以聖人猶難之。故終無難矣。

SIXTY THREE

Act by not acting.
Do by not doing.
Taste by not tasting.
By seeing small as great,
And few as many,
One can repay injury with Profound Virtue.

Confront the difficult while it is still easy.
Achieve the great by attending to the small.

The most difficult thing in the world was once easy.
The greatest thing in the world arises by starting small.
The wise one does not attempt anything great,
And yet achieves greatness.

Quick promises do not insure much faith.
Those approaching everything as if easy,
Will find much difficulty.
The wise one approaches everything as if difficult,
And therefore finds no difficulty.

六十四章

其安易持其未兆易謀其脆易泮其微易散爲之於未有。治之於未亂。合抱之木生於毫末。九層之臺起於累土千里之行始於足下爲者敗之。執者失之。是以聖人無爲故無敗。無執故無失。民之從事常於幾成而敗之。慎終如始則無敗事。是以聖人欲不欲不貴難得之貨。學不學復衆人之所過。以輔萬物之自然而不敢爲。

SIXTY FOUR

Peace and security are easy to preserve.
Trouble is easily averted before bad signs appear.
Brittle things are easy to break.
Small things are easy to scatter.
Confront them before they are obvious.
Establish order before there can be confusion.

A tree too big to embrace was once a tiny sprout.
A tower nine stories high begins with a shovel of earth.
A journey of a thousand miles begins beneath the first step.

Quick action prompts failure.
Quick seizure prompts losing grip.
The wisest one attempts nothing, and so fails nothing;
Does not hold on to anything, and therefore loses nothing.

Failure often comes on the verge of success.
As much care should be given to the end as to the beginning.
This prevents failure.

Therefore, the wise one desires only to be free of desire;
Does not esteem precious objects;
Learns not to learn the ideas of others;
And so, leads people back to correctness,
And helps all things to find their true natural path
By not doing anything to interfere.

六十五章

古之善爲道者，非以明民，將以愚之。民之難治，以其智多。故以智治國，國之賊；不以智治國，國之福。知此兩者，亦稽式。常知稽式，是謂玄德。玄德深矣，遠矣，與物反矣，然後乃至大順。

SIXTY FIVE

Long ago, those who knew of the Way
Did not try to enlighten others,
But instead allowed them to simply exist.
For when do people become difficult to govern?
When they become too clever.

Governing with cleverness robs the community.
Governing without cleverness is a blessing to the community.
In these two, one sees a pattern.
To understand this pattern is to know what is called
Mysterious Virtue.

Mysterious Virtue runs so deep and so far,
That it returns from all things,
And brings them into great Oneness.

六十六章

江海所以能爲百谷王者，以其善下之，故能爲百谷王。是以欲上民，必以言下之。欲先民，必以身後之。是以聖人處上而民不重，處前而民不害，是以天下樂推而不厭。以其不爭，故天下莫能與之爭。

Sixty Six

Why are the river and sea the rulers
Of a hundred valleys and streams?
They are good at remaining lower,
And therefore the rulers of a hundred valleys and streams.

And so, the wisest one rules by speaking with humility.
The way to lead people is to follow them.
The way the wise one rules, no one feels oppressed,
And upon taking the front position, no one feels duress.
And so the entire world never tires of giving its support.

The wisest one does not compete,
And therefore has no competition.

六十七章

天下皆謂我道大似不肖。夫唯大故似不肖若肖久矣
其細也夫。我有三寶持而保之。一曰慈二曰儉三曰不
敢爲天下先慈故能勇儉故能廣不敢爲天下先故能
成器長今舍慈且勇舍儉且廣舍後且先死矣夫慈以
戰則勝以守則固天將救之以慈衛之。

140

SIXTY SEVEN

The entire world considers my way to be great,
Yet different from all else.
Because it is great is exactly why
It is different from all else.
If it was like anything else,
It would still be small from long ago.

There are three treasures I hold and cherish:
The first is compassion;
The second is moderation;
And the third is daring to not be in front of the world.
Compassion builds courage;
Moderation builds generosity;
By not being in front, one can conduct the entire orchestra.

Now, by seeking to be brave without compassion,
To be generous without moderation,
Or to lead without humility,
One invokes death.

With compassion comes victory in conflict,
And strength in defense.
It is with compassion that heaven saves and protects.

六十八章

善為士者不武。善戰者不怒。善勝敵者不與。善用人者為之下。是謂不爭之德。是謂用人之力。是謂配天古之極。

SIXTY EIGHT

A good soldier is not aggressive.
A good fighter does not anger.
A good victor is not vengeful.
A good employer serves below others.

This is known as the Virtue of nonconfrontation.
This is putting the talents of others to good use.
From long ago, this has been known as
Being united with heaven.

六十九章

用兵有言。吾不敢爲主而爲客。不敢進寸而退尺。是謂行無行。攘無臂。扔無敵。執無兵。禍莫大於輕敵。輕敵幾喪吾寶。故抗兵相加。哀者勝矣。

SIXTY NINE

The negotiators have a saying:
"It is better to be the guest than the host.
It is better to retreat a foot than advance an inch."

This is called advancing without moving;
Rolling up the sleeves without baring the fists;
Subduing the enemy without confrontation.

There is no greater danger than underestimating an adversary.
Underestimating an adversary could mean
      losing what one treasures.

Therefore, when adversaries meet,
the one of sorrowful compassion will be the victor.

七十章

吾言甚易知，甚易行。天下莫能知，莫能行。言有宗，事有君。夫唯無知，是以不我知。知我者希，則我者貴。是以聖人被褐懷玉。

SEVENTY

My words are easy to understand,
And easy to practice,
Yet no one in the world understands them,
Or practices them.

My words come from ancient times.
My actions are subject to this authority.
People who do not understand this
Do not understand me.

Those who know me are few.
In this, I am honored.

This is why the wisest ones wear unrefined clothing,
While carrying the gem in their hearts.

七十一章

知不知上。不知知病。夫唯病病，是以不病。聖人不病，以其病病，是以不病。

SEVENTY ONE

Knowledge of ignorance is healthy.
Ignoring knowledge is sickness.

When one becomes sick of sickness,
One is no longer sick.
The wisest ones are not sick,
Being sick of sickness.
That is why they are healthy.

七十二章

民不畏威則大威至。無狎其所居無厭其所生夫唯不厭。是以不厭是以聖人自知不自見自愛不自貴故去彼取此。

SEVENTY TWO

When people lose their sense of awe,
Disaster is lurking.

Do not intrude in their homes.
Do not interfere with their livelihoods.
Not feeling your weight upon them,
They will not tire of you.

Therefore, the wisest one is self-knowing,
But does not show others;
Is self respecting, but seeks no respect;
Chooses the one in favor of the other.

七十三章

勇於敢則殺。勇於不敢則活。此兩者或利或害。天之所
惡孰知其故。是以聖人猶難之。天之道，不爭而善勝。不
言而善應。不召而自來。繟然而善謀。天網恢恢。疏而不
失。

158

SEVENTY THREE

One brave enough to attack will be killed.
One brave enough to retreat will live.
Which kind of bravery is good,
And which harmful?
Some things are offensive in heaven.
Do you know why?
Even the wisest ones are unsure of some things.

The way of heaven does not attack,
And yet overcomes;
Does not speak, and yet is answered;
Does not evoke, yet gets response;
Is relaxed, yet completes the goal.

Heaven's net is vastly wide.
Its mesh is large, yet nothing slips through.

七十四章

民不畏死。奈何以死懼之。若使民常畏死而爲奇者，吾得執而殺之，孰敢。常有司殺者殺。夫代司殺者殺，是謂代大匠斵。夫代大匠斵者，希有不傷其手矣。

SEVENTY FOUR

When people lose their fear of death,
It is of no use to threaten them with death.

If people fear death, and breaking the law
    means sure death,
Who would break the law?

There is already an executioner.
One who kills in the executioners place
Is like one who cuts wood in the master carpenter's place.
Of those who cut wood for the master carpenter,
Few escape with their limbs.

七十五章

民之饑，以其上食稅之多，是以饑。民之難治，以其上之有爲，是以難治。民之輕死，以其求生之厚，是以輕死。夫唯無以生爲者，是賢於貴生。

SEVENTY FIVE

Why do the people starve?
Because the rulers consume the wealth in taxes.
Of course the people are starving.

Why do the people rebel?
Because the rulers interfere in their lives.
Of course the people are rebellious.

Why do the people have no regard for death?
Because the rulers demand so much of their lives.
Of course they have no regard for death.

Living on nothing,
One becomes a true example of the value of life.

七十六章

人之生也柔弱。其死也堅強。萬物草木之生也柔脆。其死也枯槁。故堅強者死之徒。柔弱者生之徒。是以兵強則不勝。木強則兵強大處下。柔弱處上。

SEVENTY SIX

At birth, a person is soft and supple.
At death, a person is hard and stiff.
Young plants are tender and moist.
In death, they become brittle and dry.

Therefore, the brittle and stiff walk with death.
The tender and soft walk with life.

And so, a strong, inflexible army is easily beaten.
A stiff, unbending tree is easily felled.

The hard and strong shall fall.
The soft and weak will rise.

七十七章

天之道其猶張弓與。高者抑之下者舉之。有餘者損之。不足者補之天道損有餘而補不足人之道則不然。損不足以奉有餘孰能有餘以奉天下。唯有道者是以聖人爲而不恃功成而不處其不欲見賢。

166

SEVENTY SEVEN

The Way of heaven is like testing a bow.
As the top bends down,
And the bottom bends up,
A string too long is shortened,
And a string too short is lengthened.

The Way of heaven takes where there is too much,
And gives where there is not enough.
The way of mankind is different.
It takes where there is not enough,
To give to where there is already too much.

When people have too much,
Who will give the excess to help the world?
Only those following the Way.

And so, the wisest one works without recognition;
Accomplishes the goal without taking credit;
And does not draw attention to the value of this.

七十八章

天下莫柔弱於水。而攻堅強者莫之能勝。其無以易之。弱之勝強，柔之勝剛，天下莫不知，莫能行。是以聖人云。受國之垢，是謂社稷主。受國不祥，是謂天下王。正言若反。

168

SEVENTY EIGHT

Under heaven, nothing is more supple and yielding
   than water.
Yet for overcoming the strong and hard,
There is nothing better;
It has no equal.

Weakness can overcome strength.
The yielding can overcome the solid.
All people under heaven know this,
Yet none practice it.

Because of this, the wisest one says;
"One who takes responsibility
   for the humiliation of the people
   is fit to control the grain and earth of the community.
One who takes responsibility
   for the disasters of the community
   is fit to rule the universe."

The truth often sounds contradictory.

七十九章

和大怨必有餘怨。安可以爲善是以聖人執左契而不責於人。有德司契無德司徹天道無親常與善人。

SEVENTY NINE

When compromise ends a conflict,
Yet resentment remains,
How can this resolution be good?

Therefore, the wise one accepts the short end of the stick,
And makes no demands upon others.

One of Virtue fulfills the bargain.
One without Virtue demands fulfillment by others.

The Way of heaven is impartial.
It always accepts people as good.

八十章

小國寡民。使有什伯之器而不用。使民重死而不遠徙。雖有舟輿無所乘之。雖有甲兵無所陳之。使人復結繩而用之。甘其食。美其服。安其居。樂其俗。鄰國相望雞犬之聲相聞。民至老死不相往來。

172

EIGHTY

One should find a small community of few people,
Where people work with their hands,
And modern machines are not needed.
The people respect death,
And so are content to stay where they are.
Although there are vehicles and boats,
They have no need of them.
Although there are weapons,
They are not on display.

People should return to reckoning by tying knots.
Their food is simple but good;
Their clothes are plain but beautiful;
Their homes are unadorned yet secure;
And they are happy with their lives.

Although they are within sight of their neighbors,
And hear their cocks crowing and dogs barking,
They are content to age gracefully and die,
And leave each other in peace.

八十一章

信言不美美言不信善者不辯辯者不善知者不博博
者不知聖人不積既以爲人已愈有既以與人已愈多
天之道利而不害聖人之道爲而不爭。

174

EIGHTY ONE

Words of truth need not be pleasant.
Words of pleasure need not be true.
Goodness has no arguement.
Argument has no goodness.
Those who understand are not scholars.
Those who are scholars do not understand.

The wisest one does not possess.
The more one does for others,
The more one is fulfilled.
The more one gives to others,
The more one has.

The Way of heaven benefits without harm.

The Way of the wise accomplishes without effort.

Laotzu and the Tao

Out of the vast body which has been written about the man now called Laotzu, only a vague picture of the real person behind the book, The Tao Teh Ching, can be seen.

Although some say that he never existed, and that the work is merely a compilation of the ancient wisdom spoken to each new generation until finally written down, I think it is obvious that Laotzu _was_ that compiler, and he admits it. He constantly quotes the sayings of old, and does not take credit for originating any of the ideas he writes of.

The proof of his existence lies in his use of this knowledge, and his practice of the Tao in his writing. He is not a scholar of the Tao, but instead is one with the Tao. This insight was used to bind the ancient knowledge into a handbook for leaders — a path to follow; And thus, by following, leading.

Laotzu was the perfect candidate to write The Book of the Tao: Keeper of the Royal Archives, and so at access to much ancient knowledge; and an exception in his time — a true possessor of insight into the infinite.

A half century older than Confucius, and a half millennium older than Jesus Christ and Gautama Buddha, Laotzu was the first to put to writing some of the most enduring and pervasive ideas prevalent in every major religion on earth today.

The family of religions derived from Christianity and Buddhism form the Yin-Yang of earthly religion, yet Taoism is the vital breath which links them. It is the Spirit which completes the Trinity, and links the East and West.

"Why has the Tao been so valued for so long?
Is it not because those who ask, receive,
And those who sin are forgiven?
This is why it is so treasured by all under heaven."

For the scholars:

This edition is intended not so much for those studying the Tao, but for living the Tao. However, for those desiring the information, this translation was made predominantly from the Wang Pi edition, with some widely accepted modifications, including consideration of the Ma-wang-tui manuscripts.

The discovery of the Ma-wang-tui silk scrolls in 1973 provided invaluable additional clarity into the origins of the two books which became the Tao Teh Ching. Concerning the chapter sequence, however, by reading the chapters in the order of the Ma-wang-tui manuscripts, it becomes clear why they have evolved into their present order/disorder.

The work is not a narrative or neccesarily sequential, so the chapter order is not extremely important, but in order to understand Teh, one must first understand the Tao. Teh is contained within the Tao, and thus, it is proper that the Teh Ching take the lower position.

Acknowledgments

I would like to thank Arne McConnell and Todd Rutt, who each introduced me to the Tao in their own way; Mickey Stellavato, who made a gift of my first Tao Te Ching – by Gia-Fu Feng and Jane English (a beautiful version); Diana Warren, for proofreading the various manuscripts and providing support; And Sharyn Cunningham and Donna Chester, who helped necessitate the completion of this work, as well as provided the forum to present it to the public.

The Chinese printing contained herein first appeared in the Lao Chieh Lao edition compiled by Ts'ai T'ing Kan, which was published privately in 1922, but was not used exclusively as the translation source.

And with this edition, I would like to thank my wife, Brenda Lee Warren, who is my main support and the reason I am able to remain vertical. May our love grow for the next forty years like it has for the past twenty. I love you, Honey!

Woodblock carving, block printing and
English calligraphy by Roger Charles Warren

FIRST PRINT before final carving
of Cover Wood Block. 1993

Made in the USA
Columbia, SC
16 October 2024

44496595R00109